Soulful Season

A guided journal to help you navigate Lent.

Simon Lawrenson

DEDICATION

To the woman who rolls her eyes at my cheesy jokes and who tolerates my sock-strewn chaos.

You're the reason why our home smells like love and not mouldy coffee cups.

Thanks for not laughing at my first draft.

CONTENTS

ACKNOWLEDGMENTS

Bethany, Cookie, and Johnboy. These are my grammar wranglers, typo devourers, and flow magicians who saved my book from a literary car crash. This one's for you!

(P.S. Cookie: flawless edits, questionable singing. Love ya.)

SECTION A: THE PHILOSOPHY OF PIZZA: A SLICE OF WISDOM THAT'S EASY TO DIGEST

1. PUTTING ON YOUR SUNDAY BEST

My earliest memories of church were my two brothers and I, dressed in our "Sunday Best", sitting on a wooden pew in an old strict Baptist Chapel that had been founded in 1814. It was "the Lord's Day". My faithful parents had packed us into their Hillman Hunter estate, strategically distancing us to avoid any brotherly confrontation. We then drove the short distance to church. We would sing from the old "Sanky" hymnal (I can still smell the musty worn-out pages), accompanied by an organ. We would read from the "Authorized" King James Version Bible, and listen whilst the preacher talked for what seemed to be eternity (at least for a toddler in uncomfortable clothes).

There was a depth to it, but we didn't talk about Lent.

Over the years I had many other church experiences but none of them, at least to my knowledge, ever talked about Lent. My next significant church experience didn't come until I was 20. I stumbled upon the beginnings of a new church that was being started by a group of Americans from southern California. They belonged to a church movement that had been started in 1965 during the hippy revival. Their meetings were significantly different from how I had previously experienced church: they were quite happy sitting on the floor, dressed in t-shirt and shorts, singing simple repetitive songs led by a singer and a guitarist. The preacher spoke for about an hour and then they sang some more songs.

There was a different kind of depth to it, but we still didn't talk about Lent.

I am not alone. According to a 2017 Lifeway survey[1] while some American Christians do give up chocolate or another favourite food or drink, most simply give up Lent. 76% of those surveyed reported that they do not typically observe Lent.

Scott McConnell, executive director of Lifeway Research writes: "Lent is not about having your best life now. Those who observe it believe they are giving up things they want in order to focus on what God wants. There's little popular appeal in that."

The danger, I suppose, is that what often accompanies Christian practices like fasting, is an emptiness that, as the Apostle writes" has "the form of godliness but denies its power" [2] This means keeping up a performance that makes everything look like it's religious on the outside but rejecting that it has any power to influence the heart and mind on the inside. I would argue that there is a danger in this, and that is that relational reality with Jesus gets replaced by a religious monotony and a kind of nod to a religious monument that was long ago erected but now stands alone. So, I feel that the first thing that really needs talking about is our "Sunday Best". I've always thought that the term was about "dressing to impress". What looks good on the outside but it's just "Sunday Best". At least, that's how I used to understand the term. Growing up my Sunday Best was a shirt and tie, trousers, and super

---

[1] https://news.lifeway.com/2017/02/15/giving-up-lent-for-lent/
[2] 2 Timothy 3:5 (CSB)

uncomfortable shoes. We were only allowed to wear the outfit on Sunday to go to church but that's all. I always associated this term with what Paul writes about and it became, for me, a derogatory phrase that really means "hypocrite". However, recently I've come to understand that the term hails from the USA during the Segregation Era of 1900-1939 when African Americans attended church in their best clothes as a way of demanding acceptance, freedom, and full inclusion in the narrative of the Nation. By putting on your "Sunday Best" you are showing your community that you are serious, and that you should be taken seriously.

If my church experiences have taught me anything it's taught me the importance of being serious about my relationship with God. About being true to God and the reality of one's own relationship with Him. To have a relationship that is real, and not fake. In a word, it's putting on my genuine "Sunday Best".

WHAT IS LENT ABOUT?

For those of you, like me, who didn't grow up Catholic or Church of England, and perhaps are still yet to understand what Lent is about let me help:

As a musician I understand that occasionally, in the flow of the music, the composer will introduce a pause. A brief interruption to the movement of music where all the performers hold on a note, or stop on a rest, before moving on to play the remainder of the music. The idea is that when we pause, we are drawing attention to the fact that we have stopped. And something is coming. We are preparing the audience for what is ahead. Done effectively this will often radically alter the quality of what is coming up.

Lent is an intentional pause. It is The Composer's way of telling us, in the commotion and hullabaloo of every day, to pause and slow down. It's a pause that lasts for forty days and it is designed to be purposefully juxtaposed to our fast and furious pace of our modern lives. It is an opportunity for Christians to slow down, to look ahead, and on Easter Sunday morning, to receive a renewed joy in the Resurrection of Jesus Christ.

Lent's origins can be traced back to around the fourth century when the Council of Nicaea suggested that Christians should have a time to spiritually prepare for Easter, the celebration of Jesus Christ's resurrection. Although the forty-day duration echoes the forty days Jesus spent fasting in the wilderness, the biblical significance of the number forty should not escape us:

- In Genesis, the flood that destroyed the earth was brought about by forty days and nights of rain.
- When the Israelites were rescued from Egypt, they spent forty years in the wilderness before reaching the Promised Land.
- Before Moses went up Mount Sinai to receive the Law, he fasted for forty days.
- Elijah went forty days without food or water at Mount Horeb
- In Jonah, the inhabitants of Nineveh were given forty days to turn to God.
- Between the Resurrection and the Ascension there are forty days.

Lent is not merely a historical re-enactment on these Biblical stories; lent is a deliberate pause in the cacophony of everyday life, inviting us to engage in a profound internal journey. Let me give you Sophie as an example: Sophie decides to observe Lent by giving up coffee for forty days. Every time she is reminded of coffee, she is also reminded of what Jesus gave up for her. She is reminded to be thankful for the gift of salvation. As she looks forward, she takes joy in the Risen Jesus who doesn't require sacrifice from us but is Himself the Sacrifice for us so that we would be accepted by God.

In Sophie's world; and in our world: a society that is grappling with rapid change, social upheaval, and a pervasive sense of disconnection, the yearning for renewal is palpable. We see it almost everywhere we go: the popularity of mindfulness practices, the rise of wellness retreats, the growing interest in self-help literature, the rise in health-related diets. It seems that we are, collectively, searching for solace, for meaning, for a way to reconnect with ourselves and our deepest values. Lent, in its essence, offers a way for Christians to step off the treadmill, and for forty days strip away the distractions, the noise, and the busyness that often obscure our inner lives. It's an opportunity for us to reclaim control over our choices and put on our "Sunday Best" – to remind ourselves again that we are serious about living the Christian life.

The significance of Lent, however, goes beyond individual transformation. It is a reminder that hope, and renewal is always possible. Jesus said to Nicodemus "You must be born again"[3] and the phrase shocked him. Not because of the physical absurdity of being born twice but because he knew what Jesus really meant: that someone who had messed up and wondered far from God could come back to Him. That the spiritual impossibility of rebirth could be his. As we journey these forty days, we are ultimately drawn towards the radiant light of Easter and the promise of resurrection, of new beginnings. This is woven into the very fabric of Lent. It is a reminder that even in the midst of hardship and challenge, the potential for rebirth and redemption exists for us all because of what Jesus did on the cross.

In a world yearning for meaning and purpose, Lent offers more than just a historical tradition. It is a timely invitation to

---

[3] John 3:3 (CSB)

rediscover Jesus. So together, let's put on our "Sunday Best" and prepare our hearts and minds for the joy for Easter.

2. GUTS ARE UGLY

One of the Lenten practices that should come with a bit of a health warning is the practice of self-reflection. This is the idea that Lent is a time to turn our thoughts and attention inward, to train the spotlight of awareness on our own thoughts, emotions, and motivations and embark on a journey of self-discovery, seeking to understand the contours of our own inner world.

Self-reflection isn't without a Biblical mandate. Jesus said in Matthew 7: "You hypocrite, first take the plank out of your own eye, and then you will see clearly to remove the speck from your brother's eye.".[4] Jesus says that there is the need to first recognise the problem in one's own life before we can see clearly enough to help others. Paul, in his letter to the church in Corinth, calls them to also examine themselves [5]. But the idea of Biblical self-reflection and examination is really to get us to align our own minds with the mind of God and to get an understanding of how God sees us rather than how we see ourselves. This is because God said to Jeremiah that the heart is deceitful.[6] That means it's not going to give us a very good

---

[4] Matthew 7:7 (CSB)
[5] 2 Corinthians 13:5 (CSB)
[6] Jeremiah 17:9 (CSB)

picture of how we're doing. If fact, the danger is that the heart will tell us we're doing ok when we might not be! Where self-reflection points inward, biblical self-reflection takes an honest account of our failures and then looks quickly to the cross for what God says about us. The Psalmist calls for God to "search him and to know his heart" [7]. He calls on God to be the One who does the examining. He asks that the "words of his mouth and meditations of his heart become acceptable"[8] to God.

The word of caution here is to be wise about how our thoughts can be one of our greatest accusers. Too much introspection can deceive us into thinking that dwelling on our failures is actually a healthy response to the gospel message when in fact it can undermine the gospel message. Our thoughts remind us of our failures and if we are not careful, also condemn us because of them. I don't know how often I have become downhearted because I've realised that I've failed but failed to realise I'm forgiven! Paul's warning to the church in Corinth remind us that there is a battle in the mind: "For though we walk in the flesh, we are not waging war according to the flesh. For the weapons of our warfare are not of the flesh but have divine power to destroy strongholds. We destroy arguments and every lofty opinion raised against the knowledge of God, and take every thought captive to obey Christ" [9]

Notice that last phrase: we take every thought captive to obey Christ. There seems to be a link between a war that is being fought in the unseen realm, and how we think. This is because the Gospel is a message – it is something that needs to be heard and understood. To understand it is to be reminded of our failures, but reminded also that in Jesus we are accepted by God. As Keller once said "to be fully known and

---

[7] Psalm 139:23 (CSB)
[8] Psalm 19:14 (CSB)
[9] 2 Corinthians 10:3-5 (ESV)

truly loved is, well, a lot like being loved by God."[10] That's the gospel! That God knows us more intimately than we can ever comprehend but God also loves us more deeply that we can ever fathom.

TALK TO YOURSELF

So, what to do when it comes to self-reflection? Well think about how the 19th Century Scottish Presbyterian pastor Robert Murray McCheyne puts it:

"Learn much of the Lord Jesus. For every look at yourself, take ten looks at Christ. He is altogether lovely. Such infinite majesty, and yet such meekness and grace, and all for sinners, even the chief! Live much in the smiles of God. Bask in His beams. Feel His all-seeing eye settled on you in love, and repose in His almighty arms."[11]

I love that: for every look at yourself, take ten looks at Christ. Looking to Jesus and making much of Him helps to bring gospel balance to our self-reflection. Whilst it is true that we need to examine ourselves and spend time doing so, it is a foolish endeavour to refrain from bringing in the gospel power that promises to heal, transform and renew. The truth is that God already knows the worst about you but "does not deal with us according to our sins"[12] and promises that "if we confess our sins, he will forgive us and cleanse us".[13] Only when we are secure in the love of God for us in Christ are we empowered for self-examination that is humble, confident, and fruitful.

---

[10] Timothy Keller, The Meaning of Marriage: Facing the Complexities of Commitment with the Wisdom of God

[11] Andrew Bonar, Memoir and Remains of the Rev. Robert Murray McCheyne, (Edinburgh: Banner of Truth, 1966), 293.

[12] Psalm 103:10 (CSB)

[13] 1 John 1:9 (CSB)

The practice of talking the gospel to yourself is a very helpful exercise but one that does need practice. Jerry Bridges in his book "The Discipline of Grace: God's Role and Our Role in the Pursuit of Holiness" calls it "appropriation". It means to take the truth about our failures and sins including what the outcomes of them are on our lives and those around us, and then on a daily basis speak the gospel over them. Those failures and sins now belong to Jesus who fully satisfied the requirements of the law against them and has paid the penalty for them on the cross, setting you free to love God. This is taking the words of Paul to the church in Rome seriously when he said that "there is therefore now no condemnation for those who are in Christ Jesus." [14]

The great preacher Lloyd-Jones said:

"Have you realized, that most of your unhappiness in life is due to the fact that you are listening to yourself instead of talking to yourself? Take those thoughts that come to you the moment you wake up in the morning. You have not originated them, but they start talking to you, they bring back the problems of yesterday, etc. Somebody is talking. Who is talking? Your self is talking to you. Now this man's treatment was this; instead of allowing this self to talk to him, he starts talking to himself. 'Why art thou cast down, O my soul?' he asks. His soul had been depressing him, crushing him. So he stands up and says: 'Self, listen for a moment, I will speak to you.'… The main art in the matter of spiritual living is to know how to handle yourself. You have to take yourself in hand, you have to address yourself, preach to yourself, question yourself. You must say to your soul: 'Why art thou cast down'– what business have you to be disquieted? You must turn on yourself, upbraid yourself, condemn yourself, exhort yourself, and say to yourself: 'Hope thou in God'– instead of muttering in this depressed, unhappy way. And then you must go on to remind

---

[14] Romans 8:1 (ESV)

yourself of God, Who God is, and what God is and what God has done, and what God has pledged Himself to do." [15]

GOSPEL TRUTHS

I've been justified by Jesus	Romans 5:1
I am united with the Lord, and I am one with Him in spirit.	1 Corinthians 6:17
I'm not longer a slave to sin	Galatians 4:7
I'm a child of God	Galatians 3:26, John 1:12
I am a member of Christ's body.	1 Corinthians 12:27
I have been chosen by God	Ephesians 1:3-
I have been redeemed and forgiven of all my sins.	Colossians 1:13-14
I have direct access to the throne of grace through Jesus Christ.	Hebrews 4:14-16
I am free from condemnation.	Romans 8:1-2
I cannot be separated from the love of God	Romans 8:31-39
I am confident that God will complete the good work He started in me.	Philippians 1:6
I am a citizen of heaven	Philippians 3:20
I have not been given a spirit of fear but of power, love and a sound mind	2 Timothy 1:7

---

[15] D. Martyn Lloyd-Jones, Spiritual Depression: Its Causes and Its Cure (Grand Rapids: Eerdmans, 1965/2002), pp 20-21.

I am seated with Jesus Christ in the
heavenly realm

Ephesians 2:6

I am God's workmanship

Ephesians 2:10

I can do all things through Christ, who
strengthens me.

Philippians 4:13

3. WHEN WILL I STOP SEEING MY COUCH AS A PIECE OF CAKE?

One of the main Lenten practices is that of fasting. This is not mysterious or magical – it's simply abstaining from food or certain activities for spiritual benefit. For most of us, fasting ranks right up there with walking barefoot on hot coals or stepping on Lego just for fun but it doesn't need to be anywhere near as painful! It might surprise you to know that that when Jesus was walking the earth fasting was a weekly practice. The Jews believed that Moses went up Mount Sinai to receive the Law on a Thursday and came back down on a Monday. Over the years they developed the practice of fasting every Thursday and every Monday. In the "Sermon on the Mount" Jesus said "when you fast"[16] not "if" you fast. He assumed that fasting was a regular activity performed by regular people.

So, in this chapter I want to explore six things fasting does in the life of the believer in the hope of motivating you to fast during the Lenten period.

1. Fasting brings us close to God.

---

[16] Matthew 6:16 (ESV)

When we are confused about something, or we are seeking direction about something, fasting can position you to receive God's answers to your questions. Remember Daniel? He was reading Jeremiah's prophecy that the Israelites would be in captivity for 70 years[17] and he didn't understand what he was reading. So, in order to help him focus on what the prophecy meant and to help him understand we read that he fasted and prayed. Part of the response to the call of Christ is to follow Christ in such a way that food, water, and sleep become less satisfying that being with God. Fasting reminds us that all other appetites are unfulfilling.

2. Fasting helps us master the desires of our flesh.

Paul was determined that nothing other than the gospel of Jesus would master him. He wrote "All things are lawful for me," but not all things are helpful. "All things are lawful for me," but I will not be dominated by anything." [18] So what did Paul do? He discipled his body so that this body would be his slave rather than the other way around. He wrote "But I discipline my body and keep it under control, lest after preaching to others I myself should be disqualified." [19]

As following of Jesus, we need to develop the same attitude. If God reveals that we have an undisciplined craving for anything, or we are undisciplined in an area of our lives, we need to show our flesh who is in charge and fasting is an excellent place to start!

3. Fasting humbles the soul.

---

[17] Jeremiah 29:10 (ESV)
[18] 1 Corinthians 6:12 (ESV)
[19] 1 Corinthians 9:27 (ESV)

In his book, "God's Chosen Fast", Arthur Wallis reminds us:

"Behind many of our besetting sins and personal failures, behind the many ills that affect our church fellowships and clog the channels of Christian service...lies that insidious pride of the human heart.... Fasting...is a divine corrective to the pride of the human heart. It is a discipline of the body with a tendency to humble the soul". [20]

For us to journey towards the cross, we must humble ourselves just as Jesus did. James exhorted us to do this very thing.[21] According to Wallis, fasting is a helpful way to do that. Remember when the Israelites crossed the River Jordan, Moses declared to the people: "And you shall remember the whole way that the Lord your God has led you these forty years in the wilderness, that he might humble you, testing you to know what was in your heart, whether you would keep his commandments or not. And he humbled you and let you hunger and fed you with manna, which you did not know, nor did your fathers know, that he might make you know that man does not live by bread alone, but man lives by every word that comes from the mouth of the Lord." [22]

Fasting is a really good way to clear our minds of the delusion that we don't need God.

4. Fasting prepares us for challenging tasks.

At different points in biblical history, we find people fasting in anticipation of a significant challenge. When Ezra brought the Jews back from Babylon to rebuild Jerusalem, he called the

---

[20] A. Wallis, God's Chosen Fast (Fort Washington, N.J.: Christian Literature Crusade, 1975)
[21] James 4:10 (ESV)
[22] Deuteronomy 8:2–3 (ESV)

people to fast. [23] Jesus of course, before he launched his public ministry fasted for 40 days [24]. When Paul and Barnabas received confirmation of their apostolic mission trip it was as they fasted. [25]

So, if you are facing a significant or difficult decision, or if there is a crisis in your life consider preparing yourself with a fast

5. Fasting creates empathy with those who suffer poverty and injustice.

The Jews in Isaiah's day exhibited all the outward signs of righteousness, like fasting, but God revealed to Isaiah that the fasting and religious zeal was hypocritical. Why? Because it didn't affect their hearts. They were saying: 'Why have we fasted, and you see it not? Why have we humbled ourselves, and you take no knowledge of it?' God says to them Behold, in the day of your fast you seek your own pleasure and oppress all your workers. Behold, you fast only to quarrel and to fight and to hit with a wicked fist. Fasting like yours this day will not make your voice to be heard on high." [26]

Throughout Isaiah 58, God calls for a fast that goes beyond ceremony: "Is not this the fast that I choose: to loose the bonds of wickedness, to undo the straps of the yoke, to let the oppressed go free, and to break every yoke?" [27]

A fast should make us more aware of God and more aware of those around us. If we keep our eyes and hearts open, God will reveal human needs whereby the spiritual discipline of fasting can spill over into physical benefits as well.

---

[23] Ezra 8:21–23 (ESV)
[24] Matthew 4:1-3 (ESV)
[25] Acts 13:2–3 (ESV)
[26] Isaiah 58:3–4 (ESV)
[27] Isaiah 58:6 (ESV)

6.   Fasting aids prayers

Fasting is an expression of wholehearted zeal, as we find in the book of Joel: "Yet even now," declares the Lord, "return to me with all your heart, with fasting, with weeping, and with mourning;" [28] It is a bodily expression of "God I want this THIS much!", and I'm giving up the food that my body needs to show you". Again, Arthur Wallis writes: "Fasting is designed to make prayer mount up as on eagles' wings. It is intended to usher the suppliant into the audience chamber of the King and to extend to him the golden sceptre. It may be expected to drive back the oppressing powers of darkness and loosen their hold on the prayer objective. It is calculated to give an edge to a man's intercessions and power to his petitions. Heaven is ready to bend its ear to listen when someone prays with fasting." [29]

Now, some practical things about fasting because there are clearly different types of fasts:

- **Absolute fast** that refrains from both food and water. These are rare exceptions and should be limited to a short period of time and only if you are fit and healthy.
- **Normal fast** that excludes food but includes water.
- **Partial fast** where certain foods are permitted. Daniel is an example of someone who cut out luxury foods [30]
- **Corporate fast** where at times the church leaders have called the church to fast and pray together.

---

[28] Joel 2:12
[29] Ibid.
[30] Daniel 10:3 (ESV)

- Non-food fasts that include things that don't include food such as fasting from sleep, sex, or using a car.

The important thing to remember is that God doesn't judge our fasting by the length or totality of our abstinence from food. He cares only for its effect on our hearts. Enter your fast with a strategy for how you will spend the time and what you hope to accomplish.

4. SINNERS AND SAINTS SET GOALS

Before diving into setting your goals for this year, I want to challenge the prevailing wisdom on how we set the goals that we want to achieve. You've probably heard of SMART goals (these are goals that are Specific, Measurable, Attainable, Relevant, and Time-specific). We are encouraged to use this framework all the time, whether we are setting for the grades we want in school, or the distance I want to run at the gym, or the profits I want to earn in my business, or the weight I want to lose in the next 6 months. There is nothing wrong with these goals only to understand that everyone sets goals but only a few actually achieve them. That's why I gave this chapter the title "Sinners and Saints Set Goals" because the difference between those two isn't that one sets goals, and the other doesn't. So, what is the difference? Well, the difference is in the sustaining ability to carry out a step-by-step, everyday plan so that the goals are eventually met. For example, if your goal is to lose weight over 6 months, it's not going to do you any good just stepping on the scales and measuring how well you are doing. No, you need to plan how and when you are going to lose weight. Research demonstrates that you are 2 to 4 times more likely to achieve your goals if you make a specific plan for when, where and how you will do something to reach it. For example: "Tomorrow, I will give up checking social media with my 6:00 am morning coffee in place of 20 minutes of prayer in the study."

So, with those things in mind here's a short exercise for you to work though. Remember that it's far better to have one goal that you can keep, and do well, than ten goals that are shallow and empty. Your desires for growth and renewal will be unique, so take time to for introspection. One way you might do this is to review the "Gospel Truths" section from Chapter 2 and ask yourself which one or two of those truths are the hardest for you to believe about yourself/God. Then, use that as the basis for setting a goal. So, in the example below, I know that in my own life the idea that I can stroll into the throne room of God at any moment and get His full attention is something that I can't quite grasp. I know it to be theologically or doctrinally true (it's not as though I haven't studied it enough times to see that the Bible says it's true) but my understanding doesn't quite add up to my practice. So, in an effort to really understand this one truth, my goal will be to choose something to give up in place of prayer. I will then choose when and where I'm going to do it (usually doing it at the same time as something you already do is helpful)

Gospel Truth to focus on …

i.e. I have direct access to the throne of grace through Jesus Christ.

Goal to achieve …

i.e. stop and prayer

Thing/ activity to give up …

i.e. the morning social media scroll whilst drinking my morning coffee

When / Where …

i.e. whilst drinking my morning coffee in the study

So now that you have at least one goal and a way to achieve it let's move on and talk about hospitality as a practice during Lent. Remember, true transformation lies not in dramatic pronouncements, but in the quiet, consistent steps we take towards God.

5. CALORIES, CALVARY & THE GLORY OF GOD

Hospitality is perhaps not the first thing that we think about when it comes to Lent. We tend to think about fasting and prayer rather than feasting at a party. We can forget that a major part of Lent is about serving others and what better way to do that than to open our homes up and intentionally practice hospitality. Deeper than this, however, is the understanding that food and "the table" are a way that God enacts grace to us. To explain this let me take you back to the beginning and show you how the Bible uses the vehicle of food to demonstrate the love and grace of God:

REBELLION AND EATING

In the beginning, the Bible says that the first man and woman, Adam and Eve, disobeyed God and took the fruit of the forbidden tree and ate it. The very first act of rebellion was an act of eating.

"So when the woman saw that the tree was good for food, and that it was a delight to the eyes, and that the tree was to be desired to make one wise, she took of its fruit and ate, and she also gave some to her husband who was with her, and he ate. " 31

If we know our Bible's well enough we should know that just as food played a central part in our rebellion, it should also play a central part in our reconciliation.

RECONCILIATION AND EATING

Throughout the Bible, at key moments, God sets up a "table" and invites us to eat with Him as a reminder that God isn't finished with us. Take the Exodus story as an example and how God rescued the Israelites from the slavery in Egypt. The way that the people were to escape the coming judgement was, in part, to eat a meal:

"Then they shall take some of the blood and put it on the two doorposts and the lintel of the houses in which they eat it. They shall eat the flesh that night, roasted on the fire; with unleavened bread and bitter herbs they shall eat it. Do not eat any of it raw or boiled in water, but roasted, its head with its legs and its inner parts. " 32

We all remember the application of the blood on the doorposts of the house but it's easy to forget that God, in this moment, establishes food as a vehicle for reconciliation. A vehicle that is still commemorated to this day in the meal of Passover. Then, the Bible story continues with God feeding the Israelites in the wilderness as an act of grace, and inviting the leaders of the people up to Mount Sinai to eat and drink with God. The Psalmists often write about a table for eating: The Good Shepherd "prepares a table before me in the presence of my enemies"[33] as if to say "you have lots of enemies, but you're a friend of God, let's eat".

---

[31] Genesis 3:6 (ESV)
[32] Exodus 12:7–9 (ESV)
[33] Psalm 23:5 (ESV)

Much of the Old Testament, particularly the Prophets such as Isaiah and Ezekiel, looks forward to The Lord's final return, describing it as a party with food. a symbol that John repeats in Revelation. Isaiah 25 promises that one day God's people would eat another meal on a mountain (talking about the coming of Jesus).

It shouldn't surprise us then, when we get to the gospels that Jesus almost always seems to be going to a meal, at a meal or coming away from a meal. Luke 7:34 says that Jesus himself came eating and drinking. Jesus loved to share a dinner table with people. In fact, He loved it so much that his enemies accused him of being a glutton.

Why did Jesus come like this?

Simply because eating food with others embodies and enacts the grace of God. It's God's way of saying "I knew that you blew it with the fruit, I know you've failed since, but my offer of mercy and love still remains". This is why Jesus, soon after his resurrection, one morning meets the disciples on the shore of Lake Galilee. Remember that his disciples were heartbroken at the Lord's death, not to mention their own inward disappointment that they could not stand with Him. And so, because God's mercies are new every morning [34], whilst they were in their boats fishing, Jesus is on the shore cooking them breakfast.

What a beautiful way to say, "We're friends".

We're friends with God despite the rebellion of the first fruit (and every other way we have sinned since). We're friends because Jesus took the penalty of that sin and paid the price for it Himself. An event again commemorated by a meal, as Jesus shares "The Last Supper" with his disciples, a meal that is now observed in the church as we "break bread" or take

---

[34] Lamentations 3:22-23 (ESV)

"communion". Because the penalty of that sin has been paid for Jesus now "stands at the door and knocks. He says If anyone hears my voice and opens the door, I will come in to him and eat with him, and he with me." [35]

The greatest symbol of friendship, reconciliation, and restoration that the Bible has is when two people share a meal together. And Jesus loves to show people that whoever they are and whatever they have done and wherever they have been, there is a place at the table for you.

THE GOSPEL AND EATING

The early church knew the significance of eating together as a vehicle to show God's grace. Luke's record of how the early church behaved is significant:

"And they devoted themselves to … fellowship, to the breaking of bread …" [36]

"And day by day … they received their food with glad and generous hearts" [37]

Eating caused the Apostles some organisational issues in Acts 6, some cross-cultural issues for Peter in Acts 10 and the church in Corinth received some harsh words from Paul about eating in 1 Corinthians 8. All that to say: eating together was a practice formed in the early church because they understood what it symbolised: "I'm not only going to tell you about God's love, I'm going to show you God's love".

The beauty of practicing hospitality during Lent lies in its diverse expressions. It can be tailored to individuals and

---

[35] Revelation 3:20 (ESV)
[36] Acts 2:42 (ESV)
[37] Acts 2:46 (ESV)

groups. Some ideas of hospitality have worked well in different settings, and these range from hosting weekly gatherings that include food (such as a potluck dinner) genuine connection and community. Inviting a different family over for Sunday lunch each week of Lent is another way to open your home. Remember, however, that authenticity trumps perfection every time. You don't have to worry about making your house spotless or putting on a 3-course gourmet meal. Focus on warmth, inclusivity, and conversation.

Forward Planner: names of people I'm going to love through food

Week 1

Week 2

Week 3

Week 4

Week 5

SECTION B: MY THERAPY SESSION ON PAPER: CHEAPER THAN A REAL SHRINK, SLIGHTLY MESSIER

(The journal section)

ASH WEDNESDAY

Called Ash Wednesday because in many church traditions the palm leaves from the previous year's Palm Sunday celebrations are burnt and the ashes placed on a persons' forehead along with the phrase "Remember that you are dust, and to dust you shall return."

Today's Reading ...

Matthew 6:1-21

Questions I have:

1

2

3

Slow Down:
Write out a verse from today's reading:

Reflect:

Reflect on Matthew 6:6: "But when you pray, go into your room and shut the door and pray to your Father who is in secret. And your Father who sees in secret will reward you." (ESV). Consider the hope you hold as you begin your Lenten journey, and how the Father sees what you do behind closed doors in secret places. What hope does this give you and why should you be thankful of this truth?

WEEK 1

This week we are going to meditate on the familiar story of Jesus' temptation in the wilderness. The challenge in this story is to see how much we are governed by God's Word; how much we listen to the truth of God's word against the lies of Satan and how much authority the Bible has over our lives. Each time Jesus faces the temptation He answers the accuser with quotes from the Bible. This is key for us to understand before we get too far into our Lenten journey: the Word of God must be our authority. What that means is that if there is any tension between what the Bible says and my own experience, the Bible must win every time. That means that if the Bible says one thing, and my circumstance or experience says something different, the Bible wins. When I don't feel like my sins are forgiven, and the Bible says that they are, the Bible wins and you must rest and depend on the truth that your sins are forgiven whether you feel that they are or not. When you don't feel love, the Bible says that you are loved by God and by faith we believe this. The key is that Jesus meets each temptation with the very word that we fail at - too often we fail to receive the Word of God and we decide that it is not true and that what is around us, what is happening to us, is true instead.

We listen to the things that shout the loudest which is normally our present circumstance. So, this week you'll get the opportunity to slow down and hear the truth of the Bible being spoken over you. Hear it and receive it. Because the Word is a lamp to your feet and a light to your path [38]

---

[38] Psalm 119:105 (ESV)

Daily Readings ...

Thursday	Genesis 3
Friday	Psalm 51
Saturday	Matthew 4:1-4
Sunday	Matthew 4:5-7
Monday	Matthew 4:8-11
Tuesday	2 Corinthians 10:1-13
Wednesday	James 1:13-18

Questions I have:

1

2

3

Practicing Hospitality:
Who and when will I show hospitality to this week? (recap from chapter 5)

Slow Down:
Write out a verse from one of this week's reading:

Reflect:

What temptations or trials are you facing right now in your current season of life or situation? In what ways might these be an echo of a greater desire? Reflect on this week's Matthew passages, how does Jesus' responses help our own?

Daily Gratitude

Use this daily gratitude tracker to slow down and say, "thank you." Be as specific as you can so that when you look back you are able to be thankful all over again.

Today I'm grateful for …

Thursday

Friday

Saturday

Sunday

Monday

Tuesday

Wednesday

WEEK 2

This week we are going to meditate on two stories. One is of a lonely man who was a leper, and the other is of a man who had good friends but he was paralysed and unable to walk. The latter story appears in all the synoptic gospels, making it an important event in the life of Jesus. In Mark's gospel we're told that his friends dug through the roof to get him to Jesus. If you have friends like these, you should stop and thank God for them. They are determined – they don't know that Jesus loves broken people, or that He is going to accept him as he is, on a bed. They don't know how Jesus is going to react to them gate-crashing his bible study.

But here they are.

And no sooner had they lowered their friend down is their friend walking out of the house.

Yes, walking. With his mat under his arm. The thing that was his constant reminder of his brokenness. The thing that carried him day in and day out, is now being carried as a reminder of the thing that brought him to Jesus. Broken but now healed. Can you do that? This week you'll get the opportunity to praise God for the brokenness that led you to Him and to go away rejoicing in your weakness and God's love for your in that weakness.

It's ok to be weak. Come overwhelmed with life and hear the word of Jesus – "Son, don't be afraid", don't just sit there. Don't be carried by a former life that was marked by failure and brokenness.

Daily Readings …

Thursday	Luke 5:1–16
Friday	Luke 5:17–26
Saturday	Matthew 9:1–8
Sunday	Psalm 74
Monday	Mark 2:1-12
Tuesday	Psalm 139
Wednesday	James 5:15-18

Questions I have:

1

2

3

Practicing Hospitality:
Who and when will I show hospitality to this week? (recap from chapter 5)

Slow Down:
Write out a verse from one of this week's reading:

Reflect:
Read the introduction to this story at the beginning of this chapter again. What do the words "Son, be of good cheer" mean to you? How do they shape your view of God and your own struggles? Each day return to this reflection and add to it.

Daily Gratitude

Use this daily gratitude tracker to slow down and say, "thank you". Be as specific as you can so that when you look back you are able to be thankful all over again.

Today I'm grateful for ...

Thursday

Friday

Saturday

Sunday

Monday

Tuesday

Wednesday

WEEK 3

This story of the Samaritan Woman who meets Jesus at the well in the dusty Samaritan town of Sychar is our reading focus for this week. The seemingly mundane detail in John 4 sets the stage for a profound encounter between Jesus and a woman who was spiritually thirsting and in need of living water.

Thirst, both physical and spiritual, permeates this passage. The woman toils under the midday sun, drawing water from a deep well to meet her physical thirst. It bears the weight of shame and guilt, drawing at a time of day to avoid the other village women. Yet, Jesus speaks of a deeper thirst, one that physical water cannot quench: "Everyone who drinks this water will become thirsty again" (John 4:13). This is the thirst of the soul, a longing for meaning, purpose, and connection with something beyond us.

Jesus then offers a solution: "But whoever drinks the water that I give him will never be thirsty again. Indeed, the water I give him will become in him a spring of water welling up to eternal life" (John 4:14). This "living water" is not the stagnant well water she had been drawing from, but the Holy Spirit.

The woman, intrigued, asks for this living water. But Jesus first delves into her life, revealing her hidden shame – five marriages, the current one without legal standing. This exposure, though seemingly cruel, is a call for her to acknowledge the emptiness that superficial relationships and societal expectations cannot fill.

The final verse in this section reveals the identity of the source of all satisfaction and delight: "Jesus declared, 'I am he, the one speaking to you'" (John 4:26). Jesus, the embodiment of live and grade, is the very spring of living water. By accepting him and opening ourselves to the Holy Spirit within, we tap into a limitless source of fulfillment.

The story of the Samaritan woman offers profound insights into the Holy Spirit's role in satisfying our deepest thirst. It reminds us that:

- Our deepest thirst is spiritual, not physical. We crave meaning, purpose, and connection with God.
- The Holy Spirit is the living water that quenches this thirst. He brings life, wholeness, and a wellspring of joy within.
- Jesus is the source of the living water. By opening ourselves to Him, we tap into an eternal spring of fulfilment.

In a world choked by fleeting pleasures and superficial connections, John 4:5-27 offers a refreshing message. It invites us to turn inward, seek the living water within, and experience the transforming power of the Holy Spirit. So, this week once again you'll get the opportunity to slow down and as you seek Jesus, ask Him for this Living Water, that you'll know this deep well satisfaction.

Daily Readings ...

Thursday	John 4:5-26
Friday	John 4:27-29
Saturday	Exodus 17:1-7
Sunday	Psalm 42
Monday	Ephesians 2:1-10
Tuesday	John 14:1-7
Wednesday	Psalm 51

Questions I have:

1

2

3

Practicing Hospitality:
Who and when will I show hospitality to this week? (recap from
chapter 5)

Slow Down:
Write out a verse from one of this week's reading:

Reflect:
List the places you go to find satisfaction in life? Are they like the place that the woman in the story went to or are they other places? In what places might you find the Holy Spirit this week?

Daily Gratitude

Use this daily gratitude tracker to slow down and say, "thank you". Be as specific as you can so that when you look back you are able to be thankful all over again.

Today I'm grateful for ...

Thursday

Friday

Saturday

Sunday

Monday

Tuesday

Wednesday

WEEK 4

The Gospel of John paints vibrant portraits of Jesus' miraculous acts, each carrying a deeper message beyond the physical marvel. In John 9 we read about the encounter Jesus has with a man who was blind since birth. From it comes a symphony of joy. There have been other occasions where Jesus has healed blindness. Jesus heals a blind man in Jericho, then two blind men in Galilee, then heals a man who couldn't talk or see, then heals a blind man in Bethsaida. This story takes the prize for the strangest.

Our story begins with a man shrouded in physical as well as social darkness. Blind from birth, he navigates a world inaccessible to most, relegated to begging for survival. And, in that culture, his blindness says something profound about his identity – born blind = born rejected. For him this is a terrible thing and for his parents it was shameful. Growing up he would sense things around him but not be able to see them – things that were familiar but unkind. Like the sound of children playing but never getting the opportunity to join in. Sensing his parents fear and shame as well as disappointment in knowing that he would never marry, never have children, and never have a career. He would be dependent on someone else until he died. So, he turned to the humiliating task of begging. He had figured out that the best place to ask for money was around the temple, particularly on the Sabbath, because people loved to be seen to help those less fortunate. This sabbath, however, was going to be different because Jesus was visiting the temple and, when He finally meets Jesus, one of the strangest stories follows.

I'll let you read it yourself.

His newfound sight is not merely physical; it signifies the dawning of belief, a spark of joy flickering within his soul. I wonder how long he just stood there taking it all in as light filled his vision and colours his heart. I wonder if he stood there longer, looking at the "Light of the World," who had just been revealed to him? Of course, this story is not only about physical healing; it is a picture of what happens when Jesus encounters dark places and dark people. His redemptive touch brings light that dispels the darkness and produces joy. This joy is not fleeting; it resonates through our actions, inspiring others and leaving an enduring mark on those around us. As you reflect on this story this week, be reminded that joy is the outcome of our salvation. If you, like me, find joy to be joyless and a bit of a struggle sometimes, remember that like the man born blind, you may face darkness, doubt, and challenges to your faith but when we surrender to God's transformative power in obedience, we open ourselves to the light of Jesus, our own symphony of joy begins to play.

Daily Readings ...

Thursday	John 9:1-12
Friday	John 9:13-34
Saturday	John 9:35-38
Sunday	Psalm 13
Monday	Micah 7:8
Tuesday	Psalm 36
Wednesday	1 John 1

Questions I have:

1

2

3

Practicing Hospitality:
Who and when will I show hospitality to this week? (recap from chapter 5)

Slow Down:
Write out a verse from one of this week's reading:

Reflect:
Reflect on the flow of the story in John 9, how the man went from blindness to sight, from sight to faith, from faith to joy. How might this week mirror this same flow?

Daily Gratitude

Use this daily gratitude tracker to slow down and say, "thank you". Be as specific as you can so that when you look back you are able to be thankful all over again.

Today I'm grateful for …

Thursday

Friday

Saturday

Sunday

Monday

Tuesday

Wednesday

WEEK 5

This week we are going to meditate on the incredible story of Jesus raising his friend Lazarus from the dead. John writes about a dramatic scene that is unfolding in the little village of Bethany on the outskirts of Jerusalem. One of Jesus' best friends, a man called Lazarus, lies cold in the tomb, his death casting a heavy shadow over the household. Through this story we grow in our understanding of what is about to happen later this week – as Jesus foreshadows in Lazarus what He will do in His own tomb. Not only that, but what His own resurrection means for us, as he says to Mary, Lazarus' sister: "Your brother will rise again" (John 11:23). This simple statement, sowing the seeds of hope in all of us.

The raising of Lazarus is not merely a spectacle; it's a powerful testament to Jesus' divine power and a poignant illustration of the true life he offers. This life is not simply the extension of physical existence but a deep connection with God, a wellspring of hope and purpose that transcends earthly limitations. This week we are invited to ponder the profound question: where do we find true life? The story of Lazarus reminds us that physical existence is temporary and fragile. True life, however, lies beyond the bounds of death, rooted in a relationship with Jesus.

Daily Readings ...

Thursday	John 11:1-44
Friday	2 Corinthians 4
Saturday	1 John 2
Sunday	Ezekiel 37:1-14
Monday	Psalm 22
Tuesday	Isaiah 52:13-53:12
Wednesday	Hebrews 11

Questions I have:

1

2

3

Practicing Hospitality:
Who and when will I show hospitality to this week? (recap from
chapter 5)

Slow Down:
Write out a verse from one of this week's reading:

Reflect:
What does the statement "your brother will rise again" mean to you? Read Hebrews 11:35 again and note the words about rising again. How does faith interact with life?

Daily Gratitude

Use this daily gratitude tracker to slow down and say, "thank you". Be as specific as you can so that when you look back you are able to be thankful all over again.

Today I'm grateful for ...

Thursday

Friday

Saturday

Sunday

Monday

Tuesday

Wednesday

PALM SUNDAY

Today, we remember Palm Sunday, a day etched in history with both jubilation and foreshadowing. Imagine we are walking alongside Jesus with hundreds of other pilgrims who are also heading towards Jerusalem. We're laughing with friends we haven't seen since last year whilst the kids are running in and out of the donkeys. We're heading towards Jerusalem: not towards the gleaming halls of a palace, but towards the rugged path uphill towards the Temple. Towards a city simmering with tension and uncertainty. Yet, in the air around us hangs a palpable energy, a tremor of excitement that echoes in our shouts of "Hosanna!". Matthew 21 paints a vivid picture. See the gentle donkey, a humble steed for a humble King, carrying Jesus towards the expectant crowds. Feel the sun warm your skin as you join the throngs lining the road, hands clutching fragrant palm branches, symbols of victory and welcome. Hear the crescendo of cheers, the joyous cries of "Blessed is the King who comes in the name of the Lord!" – a chorus that washes over the city, momentarily blurring the lines between earthly rulers and the promised Messiah. This isn't a day for those whispers of dissent or murmurs of doubt. Let us not lose sight of the moment. Let the cheers resonate within us, a testament to our faith and hope.

Today's Reading ...

Matthew 21:1-11

Questions I have:

1

2

3

Slow Down:
Write out a verse from today's reading:

Reflect:

Reflect on Matthew 21:5: "Behold Your King is coming to you" (ESV) Consider the grace that comes to you in this sentence. How the King comes: humble and dependable – but coming to you. Coming to all who need Him most. What hope does this give you and why should you be thankful of this truth?

HOLY MONDAY

The scene is extraordinary: a bustling courtyard with merchants selling their wares, their shouts rising above the cooing of caged doves and clinking coins. Suddenly the air crackles with an holy uncharacteristic energy as dust gets whipped up and caught in the unforeseen gust of Jesus' righteous anger. He strides into the heart of the Temple, not a pilgrim seeking solace, but a prophet wielding a whip of truth. The scene perfectly captures the echo of the eternal battle between holiness and profanity. This is not the house of God Jesus remembers, nor the oasis of peace envisioned by the prophets. It has become a marketplace, a den of thieves, where piety is bartered, and devotion drowned in commerce.

Let the fire of His words warm us and illuminate the corners of our own temple. Where within you has the marketplace taken root? Where have distractions overtaken devotion, where have petty concerns crowded out prayer? Perhaps it's the social media scroll that steals your morning quiet time, or the endless to-do list that drowns out the whispers of your soul. Today, on Holy Monday, let's feel the conviction of the Spirit's whip to burn away distraction and embrace the cleansing fire of His purification. Holy Monday is not just a historical event but a call to action. It is a reminder that our journey towards Easter Sunday begins with an internal cleansing, a clearing of the temple within.

Today's Reading ...

Matthew 21:12-17

Questions I have:

1

2

3

Slow Down:
Write out a verse from today's reading:

Reflect:

Reflect on John 2:13-22 and the words of Jesus found in verse 19: "Destroy this temple and in three days I will raise it up" (ESV). Consider how God first destroyed the body of Jesus in the tomb only to be raised three days later. What things in your own life need to die, in order that you might find life?

HOLY TUESDAY

By now the sun is dipping over the Mount of Olives and nestled among the tree is Jesus and His disciples talking about God's plans. He speaks of fig trees, barren and fruitful, watchful servants, lamps trimmed and hearts prepared, urging us to stay awake, to be ready for the Master's return, whenever it may come.

And then, He shares the parable of the wicked tenants, a chilling foreshadowing of betrayal and rejection. The story resonates in our souls, a sobering reminder that the path to Easter Sunday winds not only through triumphant palms, but also through the shadows of the Cross.

We're reminded today to be vigilant (which means to stay awake and watch). It's not a demand for anxiety, but rather a nudge towards attentiveness: seeing beyond the distractions and hearing the still small voice of His coming.

Today's Reading ...

Matthew 21:33-46

Questions I have:

1

2

3

Slow Down:
Write out a verse from today's reading:

Reflect:

Reflect on Matthew 21:42: "The stone that the builder rejected has become the cornerstone". (ESV). Consider how Jesus being rejected by the Jewish rulers, as well as some of his closest friends, means that you will never be rejected by God. What does rejection look like to you? What about acceptance? Why is this the cornerstone of faith in Christ?

HOLY WEDNESDAY

Silence. That is the order of today. Why? Simply because the gospel writers do not tell us what Jesus did on Holy Wednesday. So today is a day for silence and reflection on who God is. Because God doesn't speak in silence but through His Word, today is a good day to immerse yourself in the Person and Work of God.

Today's Readings ...

Psalm 23:6
James 1:17
Psalm 107:8-9

Questions I have:

1

2

3

Slow Down:

Write out a verse from today's reading:

Reflect:

Reflect on Lamentations 3:19-23 and consider the things that the writer calls to mind. List them and the reasons they give you hope.

MAUNDY THURSDAY

The older I get, the more I realise that prayer is a refuge. It's the place that we run to because that's where Jesus is waiting for us. Even the Son of God sought solace in communion with His Father. When despair threatens to engulf us we can turn to prayer, not as a plea to escape, but as a space to surrender, to find strength and resolve. This is what we find Jesus doing in Luke 22 – not a surrender in weakness but hope that blooms in darkness. Someone once said that darkness does not signify the end, but the turning point before dawn.

Today's Reading …

Luke 22:39-46

Questions I have:

1

2

3

Slow Down:
Write out a verse from today's reading:

Reflect:
In Luke 22:42, Jesus cries out, "My Father, if it is possible, let this cup pass from me." How does this human moment of vulnerability challenge your own understanding of Jesus' nature and his relationship with God? What emotions does it stir within you?

GOOD FRIDAY

Good Friday is a paradox. It's "good" not because of joy, but because of the immense love that led Jesus to endure this suffering, the love that conquered death and opened the gates of salvation. Despite the name, on Good Friday, we stand beneath the shadow of the Roman Empires most feared weapon: the Cross. Today is not a day painted with triumphant palms, but in the crimson hues of sacrifice, a day remembered in seven last words of Jesus:

- "Father, forgive them, for they know not what they do." A testament to boundless grace, urging us to embrace forgiveness amidst hurt and injustice.
- "Truly, I say to you, today you will be with me in Paradise." A promise of redemption, even for the repentant thief, reminding us that hope blossoms even in the driest hearts.
- "Woman, behold your son...Behold your mother." An act of compassion amidst unimaginable pain, teaching us to tend to the needs of others even in our own moments of suffering.
- "My God, my God, why have you forsaken me?" A cry of human anguish, reminding us that even Jesus experienced moments of doubt and confusion, drawing us closer to his humanity.
- "I thirst." A simple plea amidst agonizing torment, a reminder that Jesus shared our physical, earthly experience, even in its most desolate moments.
- "It is finished." A declaration of victory, the culmination of his mission, reminding us that darkness cannot overshadow the light of God's love.
- "Father, into your hands I commend my spirit." A final act of surrender, a testament to unwavering faith, urging us to trust in God's plan, even when we don't understand.

Seven sayings. Seven living messages for our hearts today.

Today's Reading ...

Matthew 27:27-56

Questions I have:

1

2

3

Slow Down:
Write out a verse from today's reading:

Reflect:

Reflect on Matthew 27:46 — "And about the ninth hour Jesus cried out with a loud voice, saying, "Eli, Eli, lema sabachthani?" that is, "My God, my God, why have you forsaken me?". At this moment God the Father turned his face away from Jesus because of the sin that had been placed on Him. Consider the meaning of God forsaking Jesus on the cross and what it means for you. Why is this event so important and what does it mean for your access to God today?

EASTER SATURDAY

The stillness in the tomb hangs heavy in the air. The victory cries of last Sunday have faded. The execution cries from yesterday's trial have grown dim. Left behind is a quiet Saturday, a space between sorrow and joy. In our reading today we are introduced to two rich men who have come to honour Jesus' broken body. Their offering, though shrouded in grief, speaks volumes. For this Easter Saturday, let us too hold up an offering, not of spices, but of something even more precious: the fragrance of our stillness. Let us offer the quiet of our contemplation, the gentle hush of our waiting hearts.

In this day of in-between, we are not called to celebrate, nor to despair. We are called to be present, to breathe in the mystery of this sacred pause. Like the myrrh and aloes resting on the cold stone, let our stillness be an act of faith, a testament to our trust in the unseen. For what lies within the darkness? Not simply the cold embrace of death, but the promise of a dawn unlike any other. So, let's not be anxious. Let our quiet be a prayer of surrender, a preparation for the light that is to come.

Today's Reading ...

John 19:39-40

Questions I have:

1

2

3

Slow Down:
Write out a verse from today's reading:

Reflect:
Reflect on John 3:1-21 and in particular verse 16: "For God so loved the world, that he gave his only Son, that whoever believes in him should not perish but have eternal life. (ESV). Consider the hope you hold as you begin your Lenten journey, and how the Father sees what you do

behind closed doors in secret places. What hope does this give you and why should you be thankful of this truth?

EASTER SUNDAY

"He is risen!." "He is risen indeed." That is the traditional "Paschal greeting" and it is based on Luke 24:34 - "The Lord has risen indeed, and has appeared to Simon!" (ESV). Exactly how the saying became a common Easter greeting in the church is not known, but the meaning behind it is clear and something that should be held onto and allowed to resonate within us today. I should chase away the shadows of doubt and uncertainty that may be lingering. Why? The tomb is empty. Not because of theft, but because life has conquered death. Hope has bloomed from the barren soil of sorrow.

Easter Sunday is more than just a day of eating chocolate eggs and celebration. It is a declaration, a resounding affirmation that love is stronger than death, that hope has a face, and that darkness cannot extinguish the light that shines within us all.

Today's Reading ...

Matthew 28:1-10

Questions I have:

1

2

3

Slow Down:
Write out a verse from today's reading:

Reflect:

Reflect on the phrase from Luke 24:34. What does "He is Risen" mean to you?

ABOUT THE AUTHOR

I'm Simon Lawrenson, professional procrastinator, and very occasional writer. When I'm not staring blankly at a computer screen and drinking copious amounts of coffee, I can be found being "dad" to four amazing human beings who all inexplicably thrive despite my attempts at sabotage.

I started writing because if a talking donkey can become part of a literary sensation, surely someone who can make a sock mysteriously disappear into the void can spin a decent yarn. This book is the result of one too many espressos and a desperate need to prove ~~myself~~ that I'm only a walking hazard when crossing the road.

Author of "Advent Awakening: Finding Jesus in a Consumer World"

Printed in Great Britain
by Amazon

38066227R00050